I0113739

T R I G G E R S

---

*How to recognize and respond to
the sparks that impact our lives.*

WENDELL C. SIMS

Printed in the United States of America
Wendell C. Sims

Dedicated to the loving memory of my parents, Mr. and Mrs. Willie and Gedell Sims, and my late brother, their firstborn, Willie C. Sims Jr, affectionately known as Rick.

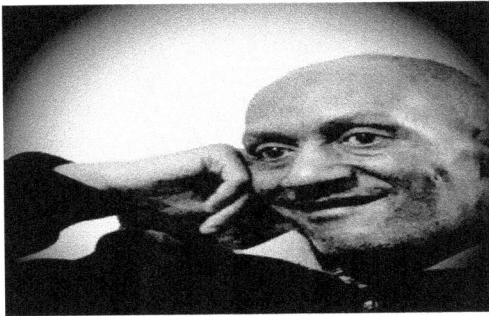

Contents

Acknowledgments

I am grateful for the people of God, colleagues, co-laborers, and to my leaders and teachers, both past and present.

I thank my pastor, Rev. Fred W. Coit, Senior Pastor of the Ridgewood Missionary Baptist Church, Columbia, SC, whose consistently calm demeanor, brilliance and resilience remain as an effective role model, leader, and ambassador for Christ.

To my beautiful beloved wife, Cynthia, whose love, patience, prayers, and companionship remain unwavering.

To my Uncle C, Louis Sims, whose experiential wisdom is "self-evident."

To the unnamed, unseen persons who struggle daily to manage the many sparks that set them off, or set them back; may you find hope, help and healing.

Finally, to the God of my salvation, who has saved me by His grace which is still amazing, His Blood that is still redeeming, and His love which is unending.

INTRODUCTION

Do you have a trigger? I have found that many people including myself have more than one. When people acknowledge their triggers, it shows great responsibility and proof that the triggers can be understood, tempered, and overcome. These pages come with the purpose of encouraging all readers to recognize and respond to the sparks that impact, enhance or hinder life at all levels.

How do I tell someone about my triggers if I don't know that I have them, or if I do not know what they are? What is a trigger anyway? Triggers are sensory reminders that cause painful memories or certain symptoms to resurface (Pedersen, 2022). Some might say, it is what sets you off. What invades your peace, imposes on your well-being, or disrupts your happy relationship? It's like the invisible switch that, when flicked, changes everything. But what happens when we don't even know where that switch is?

This journey into understanding triggers is like embarking on a quest to discover hidden treasures within us. Imagine a map with unknown territories marked by unseen triggers, and the adventure is not just about finding them but also learning how to navigate them.

Furthermore, a trigger or being triggered can serve as the lighter fluid that ultimately scorches and scars the fibers of your relationships, dreams, business, and may adversely affect your future. It's like a small spark that, if not handled carefully, can grow into a destructive blaze. Imagine how many problems could be avoided if people would know their triggers and exercise the wisdom to derail the triggers' effects by refusing to succumb to them.

I would reach full adulthood and maturity before I'd pause to recognize what are triggers and begin to identify my own. It's like getting to know yourself all over again. Discovering the things that make me react, understanding the patterns that lead to certain emotions, and realizing the power of those invisible switches.

Notably, there are several categories of triggers. The aim of this writing then is to reveal, recover, and restore through discovery what are categorically several types of triggers and how to reroute, recover, and heal from the consequences of those that are negative. We

can minimize the effects of triggered behaviors.

Chapter 1: Trauma, Tragedy, and Triumph

Trauma, Tragedy, and Triumph can all be triggers. Each one holds a different key to unlocking emotions and reactions that we might not fully understand. When I was a child growing up in Brooklyn, New York, there were "trigger phrases" that served as codes for action for the one who heard it and especially for the one it was spoken to. One example was this phrase, "Yo Mama." When and if this axiom was said in the neighborhood, it was a code phrase for a "Must Fight." Just writing the phrase honestly triggers multiple memories and could have me feeling some type of way if I am not intentionally cautious and responsible. Consequently, that was the phrase that threw two or more persons into the invisible ring to intentionally beat one another into a bloody pulp if not broken up in time.

This journey of exploring triggers and being triggered is like exploring a maze where each turn reveals a new facet of ourselves.

There are some definite positive triggers such as triumphs. A major accomplishment, a victory is a perfect catalyst for optimistic emotions, dreams, and future nostalgic memories of heightened euphoria. It's like standing on the mountaintop, savoring the sweet taste of success. However, honestly, a recent victory can also serve as a trigger for pride, conceit, self-aggrandizement, and narcissistic behavior. It's a reminder that even the sweetest triumphs can have a bitter aftertaste if not approached with humility.

I clearly remember basking in a bountiful promotion at age nineteen. I was moved from Credit clerk to Credit/Customer Service Supervisor and then Credit Manager at a major department store. All this while attending Benedict College in pursuit of a degree in education with a minor in religion and philosophy. While I didn't brag about my new positions and accomplishments, I was beaming with pride, feeling triumphant. I had power to interview people and terminate positions. However, the power was not without responsibility and accountability, which I would learn to balance these, but not soon enough. Within about a year or less, I was demoted without reason and asked to train my replacement, who was given my office before she could be trained.

Because I was still in the early stages of knowing God, I had already become familiar with some of His dealings as a voice seemingly from within my spirit said, "Pride goes before destruction, and a haughty spirit before the fall." So, then pride can and was in that case a trigger for failing or more specifically, falling. I experienced a loss of a position, status, an assault on pride which was necessary. I am only mentioning this incident here to acknowledge that there are more types of loss other than loss of a loved one through death. Some have experienced repossession, eviction, divorce, abandonment, run away pet, missing or abducted child or loved one, and the list goes on when speaking of loss; some losses may be more traumatic or tragic than others.

So, here we are, ready to embark on a journey of self-discovery, to unravel the mystery of triggers, and to learn how to navigate the maze of our emotions. Together, let's explore the categories, understand the positive and negative triggers, and empower ourselves to not just react but to respond wisely to the invisible switches that shape our lives.

In chapter two I will discuss some specific events that serve as triggers. In some ways this is a therapeutic memoir of miseries and mercies revealed in truth and trauma. I am living evidence that you can experience the traumatic and even be held momentarily in the grips of melancholy, mayhem, danger, fear, anxiety, anger, and unfair treatment. However, none of these must maintain their grip. Relief will be found as you continue discovery throughout this reading. Take a moment to reflect and even make note of areas in your life where your thinking and actions need to and will be adjusted. If you need to get into a private place for a moment to cry, trust that God will console and heal those internal wounds of the broken hearted and give you the consolation and fortitude of mind and spirit to embrace life after loss and beyond the grief and anxiety.

Chapter Two: Loss

I stood emotionally entranced, frozen in the perfume aisle of the well-known superstore. The flickering fluorescent lights overhead cast a sterile glow on the shelves lined with colorful bottles and boxes. My gaze fixed on a particular display of White Diamonds perfume, and suddenly, a floodgate of emotions opened within me.

White Diamonds—Mom's favorite fragrance. The scent that would envelop her when she wore it, a fragrance that lingered in the air long after she had left the room. I used to buy her a bottle on every special occasion— birthdays, Mother's Day, and just because. But since her death in 2021, I hadn't been able to bring myself to purchase another bottle of that perfume.

As my eyes rested on that familiar packaging, tears welled up and spilled down my cheeks. What happened? you might ask. It was the power of memory, the haunting beauty of triggers. The mere sight of that perfume triggered a cascade of grief, a poignant reminder of the woman I had lost. Though I knew she was in a better place, the memories of her life on earth were immense and profound.

This was not the first time I had experienced the weight of loss. My dad passed away in 2013, and my oldest brother, Rick, followed in 2018. The ache for one more day with them, the yearning to hear their voices, share a laugh, or witness their quirks and idiosyncrasies—it was an ache that echoed through the corridors of time.

Their voices now spoke through memories, the generational echoes, and the artifacts they left behind. In that moment in the perfume aisle, it wasn't just the scent that triggered my grief; it was the vivid recollection of moments shared, the tangible absence of Mom's physical presence.

Grief and Loss as Catalysts for Emotional Trauma

Grief and loss are powerful catalysts for emotional trauma, a storm that engulfs the soul in waves of pain and sorrow. The challenges are multifaceted. It's not only about the raw agony of the loss itself, but also about the conditions surrounding the cause of death, which can escalate the trauma.

When Death Comes

To discuss triggers is to delve into one of the most universal and profound triggers: death. Death is complex, marked by various categories and aspects of life that culminate in its inevitability.

Providential Death

For believers, there's the concept of a providential death—living a full life, reaching the biblical promise of three score and ten years, as referenced in Psalm 90 verse 10 of the Bible, and peacefully "falling asleep in death." The grief experienced in such cases is often considered "normal grief," acknowledging the fulfillment of a natural lifespan.

However, the disposition of the grieving individual is intertwined with their relationship with the deceased—the length of time known, shared history, experiences, and interactions all contributing to the tapestry of grief.

Residential Death

Residential death, occurring where one lives or lived, adds another layer of complexity. The sudden, unexpected, or violent nature of the death, especially if witnessed by others in the same residence, triggers a unique set of emotions and coping mechanisms.

Incidental Deaths

Then there are incidental deaths—those

resulting from unexpected, tragic incidents, leaving traumatized families and friends to piece together the fragments of what happened. These types may occur while in military combat, or other service-oriented careers or employment such as police force, prison guards, and others considered noble positions for which I have great respect for with the understanding that some of these positions as with others are not always held by noble persons.

Domestic violence, a disturbing contributor to incidental deaths, casts a dark shadow on many lives. According to a CDC report, more than seven people per hour die a violent death in the United States, with over 19,100 victims of homicide and 47,500 deaths by suicide in 2019 alone. In 2020, approximately 71,000 persons died of violence-related injuries in the United States. This report summarizes data from CDC's National Violent Death Reporting System (NVDRS) on violent deaths that occurred in 48 states, the District of Columbia, and Puerto Rico in 2020 (Liu, G.S. et al, 2020).

In the face of these complexities, grief becomes a multifaceted journey, a process that involves navigating the unique triggers associated with the circumstances of loss.

As I stood in that perfume aisle, I realized that the fragrance of White Diamonds wasn't just a scent—it was a trigger, a bridge between the tangible and the intangible, between the present and the memories of a past that still echoed with love and loss.

Navigating the Waves of Grief

As I stood there, lost in the memories conjured by that simple bottle of perfume, I contemplated the unpredictable journey of grief. It's not a linear path but rather a tumultuous sea, where waves of sorrow and acceptance ebb and flow. Grief, I've learned, is not an affliction to be cured but a companion to be understood and accommodated. It is a part of every human life.

The Lingering Ache of Loss

The ache of loss doesn't fade with time; it evolves. It's a perpetual yearning for moments that can never be reclaimed. The echo of laughter, the warmth of shared silence, the peculiarities that made each individual unique—all preserved in the amber of memory. Grief, then, becomes a delicate dance between holding on and letting go.

Mom's favorite perfume was a symbol of that dance. The scent held the power to transport me back to a time when her laughter resonated through the house, and her presence was an anchor of comfort. It was a trigger, not just of loss but of love—the kind that lingers long after the physical form is gone.

The Evolution of Grief

In understanding grief, I've come to recognize its evolution. It's not a static emotion; it morphs and adapts, sometimes manifesting as silent tears in the perfume aisle and other times as unexpected bursts of laughter at a shared memory. Each trigger becomes a waypoint on this journey, a marker of progress or regression.

Grief, I believe, is a testament to the depth of our connections. The pain of loss is the other side of the coin of love. The deeper the love, the more profound the grief. And so, navigating grief becomes a process of acknowledging the depth of that love and finding ways to honor it, even in its absence.

The Impact of Loss on Relationships

Loss reverberates through the tapestry of relationships, altering the threads that connect us to others. As I grappled with the loss of my mother, father, and brother, I observed how grief reshaped the dynamics within my family. Each of us carried a unique burden, and our shared sorrow forged some bonds that transcended the pain and unfortunately in reality, some distance.

Yet, grief also has the potential to strain relationships. The different ways in which individuals cope can create misunderstandings, and the weight of shared grief can sometimes feel isolating. In these moments, communication becomes a lifeline, a way to bridge the gaps that loss can create. I am here spending this much time elaborating on grief and loss, because if one does not grip their emotions they may find themselves too triggered to handle the business of planning the funeral or comforting each other who in the moment are experiencing the loss simultaneously.

Death and Its Unseen Triggers

Death, as a trigger, extends beyond the visible parameters of the physical departure. It's not merely the absence of a person but the residual effects that linger in the spaces they once occupied. A favorite chair now vacant, a silent phone that once buzzed with their calls—these subtle reminders amplify the void left behind.

Moreover, the cultural and societal expectations surrounding grief can become triggers in themselves. The pressure to grieve in a certain way or adhere to a prescribed timeline often adds an extra layer of complexity. Grief, however, is deeply personal, and its timeline is a unique journey for each individual.

I recall shortly after my dad passed in 2013, I stood in a store checkout line and while glancing down temporarily I immediately noticed the dark brown leather shoes of a gentleman who was within my father's age range. Upon further observance, these were a pair of the very same shoes that dad owned. So, I immediately left the items I had gathered to purchase, and hastily left the store in an avalanche of tears. I was temporarily overtaken with grief, but it was triggered by the seeing of those shoes a visual trigger to be discussed later.

Understanding and Alleviating Trauma

Grief, especially when compounded by traumatic circumstances, demands intentional understanding and mitigation. The trauma associated with violent or sudden deaths requires a nuanced approach to healing. Therapy, support groups, and counseling can be crucial in navigating the intricate terrain of trauma.

For those left in the wake of residential or incidental deaths, the healing process becomes a collective effort. Shared experiences and communal support serve as anchors in the storm, helping individuals find solace amid the chaos. I urge praying for and with one another especially during these times.

Coping Mechanisms and Resilience

As I reflect on the years since my loved ones passed away, I've come to appreciate the resilience of the human spirit. Coping mechanisms, ranging from a consistent faith in God, rituals that honor the departed to creative expressions of grief, offer avenues for healing.

Creating a memorial, whether through a shared space or personal rituals, has been a source of solace for many. It provides a tangible way to keep the memory alive, turning triggers into moments of reflection and connection.

Embracing the Triggers of Loss

In embracing the triggers of loss, I've learned that they are not adversaries to be avoided but guides pointing the way through the intricacies of grief. Each tear shed in the perfume aisle is a testament to the love that persists beyond the boundaries of life and death.

Grief is not an obstacle to overcome; it's a companion on the journey of remembrance. As I step away from the perfume aisle, I carry with me the bittersweet fragrance of White Diamonds, not as a trigger of pain but as a reminder of a love that endures, transcending the boundaries of time and space. And so, the journey continues, navigating the waves of grief, finding strength in the legacy of love.

Chapter 3: Triggering Trauma

Trauma can be tricky in that a previous trauma often can trigger a new traumatic experience. I believe traumatic experiences can be placed in various categories or types. For the sake of this writing, I will discuss three primary areas of trauma as they are often on the forefront of triggers: Visual, Verbal, and Violent Trauma.

Visual Trauma

A person who experienced a home fire wherein they personally had to escape and watch the remainder of their personal items go up in smoke is presented with visual wounds. That is, their eyes have seen much, and if this takes place during the pre-

35

adolescent and formative years, such trauma can have even more lasting effects difficult to reverse. The feeling of hopelessness, helplessness, fear, anxiety and anger can rush at an individual all at once or intermittently as the fire is being put out. Questions may arise and even guilt, although it may be a fire caused by electrical, lightning or some other act of nature not related to the one traumatized by it.

The aftermath and recurring flashback may keep those who have had this experience from enjoying or "warming up to" a fireplace. In fact hearing the sound of even a toy firetruck or more so seeing one can terrify. Watching movies or even television series about fires, firetrucks can be risky. Some individuals may choose to practice avoidance or implement a coping mechanism to move forward in life. However, my recommendation is to identify and acknowledge one's promptings/triggers and develop a strategy beyond avoidance to deal with it. We realistically will not be able to avoid all triggers.

Some can only enjoy a steak off the grill as long as they do not see the grill or the steak at its inception of being placed on a flaming grill. Some cannot pump gas into their car without a flashback triggered by the smell of gas. The smell or seeing lighter fluid or other paraphernalia relative to lighting even a resourceful fire may pose a problem to someone who has seen a family member, military colleague, or other loved one doused with gasoline and set on fire. Someone had to scream fire, fire!! Now there can be a verbal trigger that occurs whenever the word fire is heard or similar screaming even if it is to save someone or to avoid danger.

Visual Triggers and Tough Memories

Triggering Trauma

Sometimes, bad experiences can make other difficult things feel even worse. Trauma is like that. When something bad happens, it can make another bad thing later on feel even harder. In this chapter, we're going to look at how certain things we see can bring back tough memories and make us feel scared or sad.

Visual Trauma: Remembering a Fire

Imagine if someone had to escape from their house because it was on fire. They had to watch everything they owned burn. This kind of tough experience can leave deep scars, especially if it happens when someone is still a kid. It can make them feel really scared, helpless, and angry. Even after the fire is put out, those feelings might stick around.

When something like this happens, seeing fire or things related to it can bring back those scary feelings. It might be hard to enjoy a cozy fireplace or even play with a toy firetruck without feeling really scared. Movies or shows about fires might be tough to watch, too. Some people might try to avoid these things to feel better, but we can't avoid everything that might remind us of tough times.

Other Visual Triggers: Cars and Tough Memories

Sometimes, bad memories can come from things we see on the road. Imagine if someone was in a really bad car accident. Just seeing a car, especially if it looks like the one from the accident, can bring back scary feelings. Even the sound of screeching tires might make them feel nervous.

It's not just about the cars themselves; it's also about the places related to the accident. Driving past the spot where it happened or even hearing about car crashes on the news might be difficult. These things can be visual triggers, making someone remember something tough they went through.

I painfully yet mercifully recall an incident when while driving down North Main Street in Columbia, the smell of fire and smoke unnervingly prompted me to get out of the car and lift the hood. To my surprise my car was on fire! The severity was not great however I was not as eager to get behind the wheel and drive right after that.

Facing Illness: Visual Triggers in Tough Times

Visual triggers aren't only about accidents; they can also be tied to seeing a loved one face a big health challenge. Imagine someone close going through a tough illness, like having to get an amputation. I can recall when

Mom finally resolved to accept the medical team's advice and get an above the right knee amputation. This being a type of loss, I know was somewhat traumatizing if not for her, it ws secondary trauma for me having to witness that life changing process. The sight of a hospital room or medical equipment might bring back memories of that challenging time.

Seeing someone use crutches or a wheelchair could be a visual trigger, too. Even the sound of certain medical machines might remind someone of the hospital. It's like a connection between what we see and the feelings we had during a difficult experience. I still remember being in the hospital room with my brother when he coded and the med team rushed into his room and started the resuscitation process with chest compressions and shock, I suppose.

The Aftermath and Flashbacks: Always Remembering

After a difficult or traumatic experience, the bad feelings don't always go away. Even when things seem fine, certain smells, sounds, or words can bring back those tough memories. For example, if someone smells something like a grill, it might remind them of a fire. Or, if they hear the word "fire," it could make them feel scared all over again.

Avoiding these things might help for a little while, but we can't avoid everything. It's important to understand what makes us feel scared and find ways to deal with it. That way, we can still enjoy things we like, even if they remind us of something tough.

The Challenge of Avoiding Tough Stuff

Avoiding things that remind us of tough times can be tricky. It's important to know that everyone is different, and what's tough for one person might not be tough for another.

Finding ways to cope, even when we can't avoid everything, is an essential part of feeling better.

Verbal Triggers: Words That Stir Up Feelings

Bad memories don't only come from things we see; they can also come from things we hear. For example, the word "fire" might not seem scary to most people, but for someone who went through something tough, it could be really hard to hear. Even hearing someone scream "fire" to help or warn others might make them feel scared all over again.

Sounds like a firetruck's siren can be challenging too. It's supposed to help, but for someone who went through a tough time, it might bring back memories they wish they could forget. It's not just about seeing or hearing things; it's about how those things make us feel.

Navigating Tough Memories: Finding Ways to Feel Better

As we try to understand how things we see and hear can bring back tough memories, it's important to know we have ways to feel better. Talking to someone we trust, like a friend or a grown-up, can help. They might have good ideas on how to make those tough memories feel less scary.

Sometimes, talking to a counselor or therapist can be really helpful. They can teach us ways to feel better and not let tough memories control how we live. It's like learning how to be strong even when things feel really hard.

Conclusion: Facing Tough Times Together

Even though tough memories can make life feel tricky, we don't have to let them control us. By understanding what makes us feel scared and finding ways to feel better, we can still enjoy the good things in life. Trauma might make life harder, but with the right help and support, we can learn to be strong and

face tough times together.

Chapter 4: Verbal Trauma

A voice can soothe or scare, temper or

torment, celebrate or suffocate its listener.

WORDS

Words can bring life or death according to a

proverb I read in Proverbs 18:21. Another

slogan says "Words are powerful. How do

you use yours?" I agree with both statements, knowing that my agreement is not what makes the phrases true. Words of commendation and affirmation can encourage, inspire and direct a youngster not to give up on their hopes and dreams. On the other hand, negative, harsh, ill-intentioned words can kill one's hopes, dreams and aspirations. According to a biblical passage, [5] Likewise, the tongue is a small part of the body, but it makes great boasts. Consider what a great forest is set on fire by a small spark (*James 3:5 (NIV)*, n.d.). Children especially are influenced largely by the words of adults. A perfect example of this is found in a clip from Will Smith's 2006 movie, "The Pursuit of Happyness," has a most significant quote and scene. Particularly, in the movie, the son of the main character says while in a

neighborhood court, playing basketball; "I'm

going pro!" The character of the father

immediately responds negatively saying,

"Well, you'll excel at a lot of things, just not

this. So, I don't want you shooting this ball all

night (dlo316, 2008). In that instant, his son

throws down the basketball and begins to

pack it up in a bag. The comment made by

his father was so negative and discouraging

that it could destroy the child's dream of

becoming a professional basketball player.

The son's countenance changed, and he

appears to have immediately given up.

Thankfully, the movie continues and depicts

the main character, the father, recognizes the

fatality of his words and he then rephrases

and affirms his son with positive and confident

words encouraging him to pursue his dreams.

In fact, this father says, "Hey, don't ever let

anyone tell you, you can't do something. You

got a dream, go for it."

Chapter 5: The Ripple Effect of Broken Bonds: Unraveling the Triggers

In the annals of history, relationships, even the most sacred and steadfast, have met their share of storms. Acts 15:36 paints a poignant picture of a fracture between two devotees of early Christianity—Barnabas and Paul. The catalyst for this schism? The role Mark should play in their return to the places where they had fervently preached the gospel.

Barnabas, the son of encouragement, advocated for Mark's inclusion in their journey. However, Paul, unwavering in his conviction, hesitated. Mark had abandoned them during their inaugural journey, and for Paul, this betrayal was a wound too deep to overlook.

The Seeds of Discord: Mark's Shadow Lingers

The disagreement between Barnabas and Paul marked the genesis of a narrative threaded with broken bonds, and it sets the stage for our exploration into how such ruptures can trigger a cascade of behaviors and conditions.

Broken relationships, like fault lines, have a

ripple effect. The seismic tremors as in an earthquake are felt far beyond the epicenter of the disagreement. The decision to part ways became a trigger for a series of emotional and psychological responses.

Isolation: The Silent Fallout of Broken Ties

The first aftershock of broken relationships is often isolation. Just as Barnabas and Paul took different paths, individuals in the aftermath of a falling-out find themselves on separate emotional islands. The once-strong camaraderie replaced by a stark sense of aloneness.

Isolation can be a breeding ground for a multitude of negative emotions. It fosters an environment where the mind becomes a relentless echo chamber, amplifying feelings of abandonment and rejection.

While I was maybe in the fifth grade, my best friend and I were forced into fighting each other by those who enjoyed strife and rivalry, although we were not mature enough to understand. We both agreed to a dual after school, and in retrospect it was kind of funny to see us circling one another taking swings, and intentional missed punches because we really did not want to hurt each other. I came to realize however, much later that a dent in our friendship was made that would permanently impact our lives. Our comradery dismissed without known cause, since we ended the after school tussle having concluded that we did not know why were fighting.

Anger: The Fire Ignited by Hurt

Paul's refusal to take Mark along was not merely a logistical decision; it was an emotional response fueled by anger. Broken bonds often give birth to this intense emotion, an emotion that can scorch relationships further or become a smoldering ember, casting a perpetual shadow on future interactions.

Anger, when left unchecked, can manifest in destructive ways. It can be the driving force behind hurtful words, impulsive actions, and a widening chasm between parties involved.

Depression: The Weight of Unresolved Conflict

As the dust settled from the clash between Barnabas and Paul, it is likely that a behind the scenes sense of melancholy lingered. Broken relationships can sow the seeds of depression, a heavy burden carried by those who find themselves ensnared in the tangle of unresolved conflict.

The prolonged emotional turmoil resulting from fractured ties can lead to a deepening sense of hopelessness and despair. The unspoken words, unaddressed grievances, and lingering shadows of what once was can cast a long, looming darkness over individuals.

Addictive Behaviors: Seeking Solace in Substances

In the void left by severed connections, individuals may turn to various coping mechanisms, and one perilous path is the allure of addictive behaviors. I am certainly not saying this was the case with Paul nor Barnabas, however, just pointing out for the sakes of this writing what can and often does happen in the aftermath as being triggered by contention. Whether seeking solace in substances or addictive activities, the attempt to numb the pain becomes a misguided response to the emotional void.

Addiction, often a silent companion of broken relationships, can spiral into a destructive cycle, providing a temporary escape but exacerbating the underlying issues. What might you gravitate to in hopes of anesthetizing the pain of loss, separation, contention or rejection?

The Journey to Healing: Navigating Emotional Turbulence

The broken relationship between Barnabas and Paul stands as a testament to the emotional turbulence that can be unleashed when bonds fracture. The journey to healing is fraught with challenges, but it begins with acknowledging the emotional fallout and understanding the triggers that propel negative behaviors.

Communication becomes the compass for this journey. Honest conversations, devoid of blame but rich in empathy, can be the first step toward rebuilding bridges. Recognizing the emotional triggers and their impact is pivotal in preventing the cascade of negative behaviors.

Forgiveness, though challenging, is the balm that soothes the wounds. Both Barnabas and Paul had to navigate their own paths, yet the narrative of Acts suggests that time, coupled with understanding and forgiveness, allowed for a measure of reconciliation.

Conclusion:

The fractured relationship between Barnabas and Paul, triggered by the discord over Mark's role, is a reminder that even the strongest bonds can succumb to strain. Broken relationships just like shattering glass, send fragments across the landscape of emotions, leaving behind a complex garment of frailty and resilience.

Understanding the triggers that arise from such fractures is crucial, for in this understanding lies the potential for healing. As we navigate the tumultuous waters of broken bonds, let us not forget the transformative power of reconciliation, forgiveness, and the enduring resilience of the human spirit.

Chapter 6: Leadership Challenges: Understanding Triggers through Elijah's Story

Being a leader has its highs and lows, and sometimes, even the strongest leaders can face unexpected challenges. In this chapter, we'll explore the story of Elijah, a leader from ancient times, and dive into the triggers that may have influenced his behavior. By understanding these triggers, we can gain insights into the factors that affect leaders and their decisions.

1. Elijah's Triumph: The Power of Success (1 Kings 18)

Imagine having a day where everything you do turns out amazing. Elijah experienced just that in 1 Kings 18. He stood up against rival beliefs, proved his God's power, and ran faster than a king. It was a hero moment, a peak of success that showcased his courage and strength.

2. The Unexpected Turn: Jezebel's Threat (1 Kings 19)

But success doesn't always shield leaders from new challenges. Elijah, after his big win, faces a sudden threat from Queen Jezebel. This unexpected turn triggers a shift in his behavior, making him fearful and leading him to run away. Understanding what triggered this change is crucial for leaders facing their own challenges.

3. The Power of Threats

Jezebel's threat is a powerful trigger that

shakes Elijah's confidence. Leaders often face external threats, criticism, or opposition, which can impact their decision-making.

Understanding how to handle threats without letting them overpower rational thinking is a crucial skill for leaders. Here is where I advise leaders major on having a disciplined temperament. As a ministry leader, I have experienced and witnessed more than a few where the chronic complainers and criticizers of leadership and ministry are those who barely attend Bible study or any form of Christian education offered by the local church. Once during a moment of feeling accomplished, after concluding a series of teaching from the book of Revelation, a child asked me, "Why don't you ever teach from the book of Revelation?" I was appalled at first, but then I knew this was a question prompted by an adult who decided to use the child's voice to ask the question. Yes, unfortunately such things do occur in church sometimes. Remember, in our previous chapter, Paul and Barnabas were leaders in the mission field so they dealt with many people including friction between the two of them.

4. The Weight of Expectations

Success can bring a heavy burden of expectations. Elijah's sudden fall may be linked to the pressure of maintaining his heroic status. As a leader, I often grapple with the weight of expectations from myself and others, and this can become a trigger for anxiety and fear of failure if not guarded.

5. Emotional Toll of Leadership

Leadership isn't just about making decisions; it involves a rollercoaster of emotions. Elijah's story reflects how the emotional toll of leadership, from the high of success to the fear of failure, can be a trigger for unexpected behavior. As leaders, we need to navigate our emotions wisely to make sound decisions. There have been instances where I did not master this behavior, but thanks be to God I have the merciful opportunity of another chance.

6. Burnout and Exhaustion

Leaders often run on full throttle, but constant pressure can lead to burnout. Elijah's exhaustion after the Mount Carmel event is a trigger for his escape and desire for rest. Recognizing signs of burnout and implementing self-care strategies are crucial for leaders to avoid the meltdown that can follow prolonged stress.

7. Isolation and Loneliness

Leadership can be a lonely journey. Elijah's choice to isolate himself in the wilderness is a trigger that exacerbates his emotional state. Leaders need support systems, and isolation can be a dangerous trigger that amplifies the impact of challenges.

8. Reflection on Triggers

Elijah's story prompts leaders such as I to reflect on our own triggers. What situations make me anxious or fearful? When do I feel the weight of expectations? Recognizing personal triggers is the first step in developing strategies to navigate challenges and make decisions that align with one's leadership values. What I value most is my relationship with God. Although in some aspects Elijah may be perceived as a wimp to some in taking flight from Jezebel, he is quite heroic and a primary exemplar of leadership in that he did recognize God's voice, held candid communication with God, acknowledged and voiced his fears. What are your triggers and how are you dealing with them?

Conclusion

Leadership is a dynamic journey filled with challenges and triumphs. Elijah's story illustrates that even the strongest leaders have triggers that can influence their behavior. By understanding these triggers—whether they stem from external threats, internal pressures, emotional toll, burnout, or isolation— as leaders we can equip ourselves to navigate the complexities of our roles. The ability to identify and manage triggers is a vital skill that empowers leaders to make wise decisions even in the face of adversity, ensuring our journey is one of growth and resilience.

Chapter 7: The Echoes of Rejection

Growing up in Brooklyn, New York, there were days that left a mark on my heart, like a tattoo etched with the ink of rejection. One such day, when I was around nine, stands out vividly in my memory.

It was a sunny afternoon, the kind that makes the streets of Brooklyn come alive with the chatter of neighbors and the distant melody of an ice cream truck. I was filled with the innocent curiosity that only a child possesses, eager to explore the world around me. My dad, a towering figure in my small world, was getting ready to go somewhere. His movements were deliberate, and I could sense an air of mystery surrounding his departure.

As I watched him gather his belongings, I mustered the courage to ask, "Dad, where are you going? Can I come too?" I was met with a response that would become a haunting echo in the corridors of my mind, "Nunya," he said, the word unfamiliar and cold. Confused, I asked what it meant, and he replied, "None of your business." The dismissive tone struck me like a sudden gust of wind, knocking the breath out of my sails.

Undeterred, I persisted, trailing behind him like a persistent shadow. "Can I come, please?" I pleaded, hoping for a glimpse into the mysterious world my father was about to enter. His gaze fixed on the distance, he snapped, "Get back to the house," his words sharp and final. My heart plummeted as he continued walking, each step taking him farther away until he vanished into the bustling Brooklyn streets heading towards the train station on Eastern Parkway.

In that moment, I believe a tiny seed of rejection was planted in the soil of my young heart. The words, "Nunya" and "None of your business," became a fence, separating me from the warmth of inclusion. The rejection stung, leaving me questioning my own worth. What had I done wrong? Why wasn't I allowed to know where he was going? These questions swirled in my mind, creating a fog of self-doubt.

That incident marked the beginning of a recurring dream, or rather a haunting vision. Night after night, I would see the image of my father walking away, his figure becoming smaller and smaller until it faded into the distance. The dream mirrored that memorable day in Brooklyn, the emotions raw and vivid. Even though he always returned, the seed of rejection had taken root, and its branches cast a long shadow over my sense of self.

The dream became a trigger, a key that unlocked a flood of emotions whenever I felt a hint of rejection. It wasn't just about my dad anymore; it was a lens through which I viewed the world. Rejection, whether real or perceived, became a powerful force shaping my understanding of relationships and self-worth.

As I navigated the challenges of adolescence, the echoes of that sunny day in Brooklyn reverberated in my interactions with others. Each rejection, no matter how small, seemed to water the seed planted by my father's words. I became hyper-aware of the slightest hint of disapproval, and the fear of being cast aside crept into my relationships like a silent intruder.

Rejection, like a pebble tossed into the still waters of a pond, creates ripples that extend far beyond the initial splash. It's not just the immediate pain; it's the lasting impact on one's perception of oneself and others. In my case, the rejection from my father became a template for interpreting the actions of those around me. I developed a radar for potential rejection, always on high alert to protect myself from the pain of being left behind.

The effects of rejection are like a chain reaction. The initial event plants a seed, and the triggers, like the recurring dream of my father walking away, reinforce the belief that I am somehow fundamentally flawed. This belief colors every interaction, turning the mundane into a battlefield where I must prove my worth.

Understanding the causes and effects of rejection is a journey, a process of unraveling the threads that bind us to past experiences. For me, it meant revisiting that day in Brooklyn, confronting the pain, and recognizing that my father's words were not a measure of my value. They may have reflected his own struggles and limitations.

Rejection is a universal experience, and its

impact varies from person to person. However, rejection can certainly be a trigger. The key to breaking free from its grip lies in acknowledging the pain, understanding its origins, and rewriting the narrative that plays in the recesses of the mind. It's about recognizing that rejection, though painful, does not define who we are.

In the landscape of the human heart, there are valleys of rejection and mountains of acceptance. Each rejection, each echo from the past, is an opportunity to draw closer to God in whom we are accepted, to climb higher, to see the world from a new perspective. It's a chance to redefine our worth and rewrite the story that rejection seeks to tell.

As I look back on that memorable day in Brooklyn, I see it not just as a source of pain but as a catalyst for growth. The seed of rejection may have been planted, but so was the resilience that would allow me to weather life's storms. The echoes of that day no longer hold the same power; they have become a reminder of the strength that lies within, waiting to be discovered.

A momentary sting or something more?

Rejection, a bitter pill that many of us have tasted, is more than just a momentary sting. It is a catalyst that can set off a chain reaction, creating triggers that reverberate through our lives. Understanding the dance between rejection and triggers unveils the intricate ways in which our behaviors are shaped by the wounds of dismissal.

The Seeds of Triggers:

Rejection plants seeds of triggers deep within our psyche. These triggers are like dormant landmines, lying in wait until something, often seemingly innocuous, sets them off. Much like the day in Brooklyn when my father's words became the catalyst for my trigger, rejection imprints itself on our emotional landscape, waiting for an opportunity to resurface.

The triggers take various forms, each unique to the individual's experiences. For some, it might be the fear of abandonment, while for others, it could manifest as a desperate need for approval. These triggers color our perceptions, influencing how we interpret the world around us. They become the lenses through which we view ourselves and others.

Behaviors Triggered by Rejection:

1. **Seeking Approval:** The need for approval is a common behavior triggered by rejection. Having once felt the sharp pain of being unwanted, individuals may go to great lengths to seek affirmation from others. This might lead to people-pleasing behaviors, as the fear of rejection fuels a constant desire to be accepted.

2. **Avoidance:** Rejection can create an aversion to situations that mimic the circumstances of past dismissals. This avoidance can be both physical and emotional. For instance, someone who

experienced rejection in a romantic relationship might avoid intimacy, while another person who felt rejected in a social setting might shy away from gatherings.

3. **Defensiveness:** The sting of rejection often leaves behind a defensive armor. Individuals may become hypersensitive to criticism, always on guard to protect themselves from the perceived threat of rejection. This defensiveness can strain relationships and hinder personal growth.

4. **Self-Sabotage:** In a twisted attempt to control the narrative, some individuals may engage in self-sabotaging behaviors. This can range from undermining personal achievements to

pushing away those who care about them. The logic is paradoxical: if you reject yourself first, the pain of external rejection is somehow lessened.

5. **Isolation:** Repeated experiences of rejection can lead to a fear of forming connections. The safety of isolation becomes preferable to the vulnerability of opening up to others. This self-imposed isolation, while providing a temporary shield, exacerbates the loneliness that rejection often brings.

6. **Overachievement:** On the flip side, rejection can fuel an intense drive to prove one's worth. The constant need to excel, whether academically, professionally, or socially, becomes a coping mechanism. Success becomes

a shield against the perceived threat of rejection, even if it comes at the cost of personal well-being.

7. **Emotional Numbness:** To shield oneself from the pain of potential rejection, some individuals develop a veneer of emotional numbness. This detachment, while providing temporary relief, inhibits the depth of emotional connections and can contribute to a sense of emptiness.

Breaking the Cycle:

Recognizing the behaviors triggered by rejection is the first step toward breaking the cycle. It involves a journey of self-discovery and introspection. Unraveling the knots of triggers requires acknowledging the wounds left by rejection and understanding that these wounds do not define one's worth.

Therapy and support systems play a crucial role in this process. A therapist can provide tools to navigate the tumultuous waters of rejection-triggered behaviors, offering a safe space for healing and growth. Additionally, fostering healthy relationships can gradually reshape the narrative, replacing the echoes of rejection with the harmonious chords of acceptance.

In conclusion, the dance between rejection and triggers is a complex one. Understanding the types of behaviors triggered by rejection empowers individuals to reclaim agency over their lives. It's a journey that requires courage, self-compassion, and a willingness to confront the wounds of the past. As we unravel the intricacies of our triggers, we pave the way for a future where rejection loses its power to dictate our behaviors and, ultimately, our happiness.

Whether actual, assumed or exaggerated, abandonment is a primary trigger for numerous counterproductive behaviors.

Chapter 8: The Domino Effect of Abandonment

In the process of unraveling the knots of abandonment, I discovered the transformative power of self-compassion. The question that once emanated from a place of fear and desperation evolved into a mantra of self-assurance — a declaration that I was worthy of love and belonging, irrespective of the actions of others.

Alright, so let's talk about that time when it feels like someone's about to bail on you, and it messes with your whole world. It's like a chain reaction of feelings and actions that get set off when you think, "Are you leaving too?" – a question Jesus asked back in the day when some of his buddies ghosted him.

Abandonment isn't just a one-time thing; it's like a pebble thrown in a pond, making ripples that touch every part of your life. So, when folks bail, it triggers a bunch of reactions, and let me tell you, they're not always the best.

First off, trust becomes this rare treasure you're scared of losing. You start second-guessing everyone's motives, wondering if they're gonna ditch you like the last crew did. It's like putting up walls to protect yourself from the possibility of being left hanging.

Then there's the whole vulnerability thing. You start thinking that if you let people see the real you, they might use it against you or just walk away. So, you put on this tough exterior, like a superhero with an invisible shield, hoping it'll keep you safe.

Abandonment messes with your choices, too. You might find yourself doing things that don't really make sense, just to make sure people won't leave. It's like you're playing a game, but the rules keep changing, and you're trying to keep up so no one decides to bail on you again.

Ever notice how some folks go all-out to be the center of attention? That might be a reaction to feeling abandoned. It's like, "Hey, look at me! Don't go anywhere because I'm the coolest person ever!" It's a way of shouting, "Please don't leave me behind!"

Then there's the flip side – some people pull away when they're scared of being left. They become the disappearing act, like they're saying, "If I go first, you can't leave me because I'm already gone." It's a weird strategy, but when abandonment messes with your head, you try all sorts of things to cope.

Now, I'm not a psychologist, but I've read about this Bowlby guy and Ainsworth lady. They say our early experiences can mess with how we handle relationships later on.

Abandonment in the past can turn you into a detective, always on the lookout for signs that someone's about to bail, and that's not the best way to live.

But here's the thing – facing those triggers head-on can be like defusing a bomb. It's tough, but it's better than letting those triggers control your life. Therapy, talking it out, and understanding that not everyone's gonna ditch you can be a game-changer.

Sure, the fear of being left behind might still rear its head now and then. It's like a sneaky character in a video game that keeps popping up. But when you recognize those triggers and don't let them dictate your actions, it's like leveling up in the game of life.

So, next time you feel that "Are you leaving too?" moment, remember, it's not just a question. It's a trigger that sets off a bunch of reactions. But you've got the power to change the game, face those triggers, and show the world you're more than the echoes of abandonment.

Chapter 9: The Dance of Anger

In the quiet recesses of our minds, anger simmers like an unattended pot left to boil over. It's a force that can consume reason, shred relationships, and burn bridges. I've always been intrigued by the saying, "Anger is just one letter away from Danger," and never has its truth resonated more profoundly than in the tapestry of emotions that pulse through our veins. As I reflect on the impact of anger, I'm compelled to unravel the intricate dance between this volatile emotion and the triggers that set it ablaze.

Anyone who works in the public sector with people should and must control their temperament. I can remember in a childhood fit of rage, (it pains me to even write this), and

I also know that some will race to judge me, but I am not concerned about that, I slammed the door as my mother was walking out of our apartment home in Brooklyn. Her exit happened to take place after she had given several "bossy" directives including announcing that one of my older siblings would be in charge until she returned from some sort of outing. I could feel my body temperature go up and if it were possible, smoke would have protruded out of my ears. The problem was not just me slamming the door, it was the scream I heard on the other side of the door when it slammed. Yes, if you're thinking it, you are right, in my fit of rage, I had unintentionally slammed Mom's hand in the door. Besides the emotional guilt and sorrow that engulfed me for doing that, corporal punishment ensued, I suppose she accomplished it with the unscathed hand. I saw stars that night! I did learn a valuable lesson that anger is just one letter away from danger. While I wanted to slam the door, I never in a million years wanted to harm my mother in any way. I do not believe I have slammed any doors since then. As a matter of fact, I could say hearing or seeing someone slam a door can trigger a flashback of emotions.

This is a good place to get your mind off my infraction and do a little self reflection and evaluation. What angers you? How do you handle your anger? Do you experience "road rage?" Can you say that you are disciplined in this part of your life? What happens when things don't go as you planned or as you

desire, and who is the recipient of your rage?

If you are struggling in this area, I recommend

a study of the fruit of the spirit as found in

Galatians 5:22, and temperance.

Chapter 10: The Tumultuous Tango of Triggers

Anger is a chameleon, assuming various shades and intensities based on the triggers that beckon it forth. Triggers, like hidden tripwires, can be as inconspicuous as a misspoken word or as blatant as a betrayal. They lurk in the shadows, ready to pounce on the slightest provocation. In my journey through the maze of emotions, I've come to realize that understanding these triggers is akin to deciphering a cryptic code—one that holds the key to taming the tempest within.

Mark B. Powell, an astute observer of human behavior, points out the intriguing interplay between personality types and their relationship with anger. According to Powell,

Thinkers, in contrast to Feelers, may find themselves unwittingly entangled in situations that trigger their anger. These individuals, characterized by a penchant for logic and analysis, may overlook the nuances of their emotions. They might bypass the crucial self-reflection needed to comprehend what ignites their inner fury.

Thinkers, Powell notes, may tread through life with a casual indifference to the emotional intricacies that underlie human interactions. This indifference, while a testament to their analytical prowess, can render them vulnerable to explosive bouts of anger. It's as if their emotional development has frozen in time, leaving them to react to provocations with the impulsive rage of a child.

The Unexplored Depths of Feelers

Contrastingly, Feelers navigate the emotional landscape with a nuanced sensitivity. They invest time and effort in understanding the tapestry of their feelings—knowing what stirs joy, triggers sorrow, and kindles the flame of anger. Powell's insights shed light on the stark disparities between Thinkers and Feelers in managing their emotional arsenal.

Feelers, he suggests, are adept at decoding the intricate tapestry of relationships. They invest in the emotional groundwork necessary for robust connections. Unlike their Thinker counterparts, Feelers tend to be more in tune with their emotional landscape, aware of the triggers that can set off a storm within. It's a testament to their commitment to relationships

and a stark contrast to the emotional
detachment that Thinkers may exhibit.

The Immature Outbursts of Thinkers

Thinkers, in their unintentional neglect of
emotional development, may find themselves
ensnared in the web of anger. The lack of
self-awareness, coupled with a certain
emotional naivety, can lead to outbursts that
mirror the unbridled tantrums of a child. It's a
paradox—the rational mind succumbing to
irrational fury.

In my own experiences, I've witnessed the
aftermath of such immature eruptions.
Thinkers, who may excel in the boardroom or
laboratory, find themselves stumbling in the
delicate terrain of interpersonal relationships.

Their anger, undisciplined by the wisdom of emotional insight, becomes a destructive force, leaving fractured friendships and strained partnerships in its wake. I grew up in an emotionally charged environment, where reacting versus responding was the norm. In fact often I thought you weren't considered to be in a real conversation until somebody was getting cussed out. The more profanity and vulgar language used, the cooler you were. My dad always seemed to maintain his cool. His pattern of peacefully speaking coupled with my conversion to Christ in my late teen years have helped me to avoid both the prison and the pit. I vividly remember fighting a neighbor in my childhood, who was obviously bigger than me as most were; me being one of the smallest in the family. Nevertheless, as

I think back on the incident, where the neighbor got not only beat up, but also cussed out until he ran upstairs crying likely from both, I interpreted, I don't recall what triggered the fight. Nonetheless being the victor was pleasant enough. My personality, I have discovered, is one that consists of being a thinker and a feeler, but in those early years mainly thinker. The primary thought was to win, get the victory, prize, trophy, bragging rights, or as in my elementary math class, the pencil that I won for being the first to correctly solve a math problem on the board.

The Dangerous Balancing Act

As I ponder the intricate dance between personality types and anger, I'm reminded of the delicate balancing act required to navigate the tapestry of emotions. It's a journey that demands introspection, a willingness to confront the fears and terrors within, and a commitment to understanding the triggers that lie in wait in the shadows.

In the workplace, where the symphony of collaboration and competition unfolds, the impact of unchecked anger can be particularly pronounced. Colleagues become collateral damage, and professional relationships bear the scars of emotional turmoil. The career trajectory of an individual, no matter how brilliant, can be irrevocably altered by the inability to master the dance of anger and triggers.

The Recovery of Self-Awareness

Yet, amidst the tumult, there is restoration and recovery in self-awareness. The first step toward taming the tempest of anger is acknowledging its presence. Whether one identifies as a Thinker or a Feeler, the journey begins with a willingness to delve into the depths of one's emotional landscape.

For Thinkers, this entails a conscious effort to bridge the gap between logic and emotion. It requires acknowledging that emotional intelligence is not a weakness but a formidable ally in the pursuit of balanced relationships. The journey toward self-awareness is a gradual unfolding—a peeling back of layers that exposes vulnerabilities, triggers, and the dormant seeds of anger.

Feelers, on the other hand, can contribute to

this dance by fostering an environment of understanding. While their emotional insight is a strength, it's essential to recognize that others may navigate the tapestry of feelings with a different compass. Patience, empathy, and open communication become the tools to bridge the gap, fostering an atmosphere where emotional intelligence can thrive.

Conclusion: The Symphony of Self-Mastery

In the symphony of human emotions, anger is a powerful crescendo that demands attention. Its impact, whether harnessed or unbridled, reverberates through the interiors of our personal and professional lives. The dance with anger is a complex choreography, where triggers and personality types perform in a cycle, dictating the rhythm of our responses.

As I pen down these reflections, I am acutely aware of the importance of self-mastery in the face of anger. It's a journey that requires courage—the courage to confront the shadows within, to understand the triggers that beckon the storm, and to deal with anger in a way that transforms its destructive force into a catalyst for growth.

For in the end, it is not the absence of anger that defines us, but the way we navigate its turbulent currents. It's a journey of introspection, empathy, and the unwavering commitment to mastering the dance of emotions—a dance that, when choreographed with wisdom, transforms the discordant notes of anger into a harmonious symphony of self-awareness and resilience.

Alcohol can be an agent of appreciation and celebration or an ally for abuse. While alcohol consumption can be addictive, causing alcohol use disorder, while under the influence more than a few persons have become abusive to other people and sometimes to themselves. My intent in this portion of the writing is not to attempt to settle the ongoing debate of whether or not Bible believing Christians should drink nor am I on a mission to cure alcoholism and its devastating effects. I am however assigned to provoke the thought process of the reader who may or may not be a social or habitual consumer of alcohol. Being my authentic self, I must give the scriptural warning here though, "Wine is a mocker, strong drink is raging: and whosoever is deceived thereby is not wise." Proverbs 20:1. In my pre-adolescent and adolescent years, I have seen the severely negative effects of some who were out of control with their alcohol consumption. As such they exhibited impaired motor skills, poor decision making and many unadmitted regrets. I even saw a relative drink his own urine while intoxicated... ughghh!! Talking about out of control! So, then alcohol consumption can and often does serve as a trigger for other behaviors.

Chapter 11: The Liquid Rollercoaster: Unleashing Chaos

Alright, so imagine this golden liquid in a glass or sometimes it's clear liquid, but it wasn't water—booze, spirits, liquor, the hard stuff. It smells strong, and it's like the life of the party, making everything more fun. But here's the deal: it's got a dark side too, and that's what we're getting into. I'm not trying to tell you what to do, but there's this saying, "Wine is a mocker, strong drink is raging: and whosoever is deceived thereby is not wise" (Proverbs 20:1). Just keep that in mind.

Growing up, I saw some seriously messed-up stuff with people going crazy with this drink. Picture this: a family member who used to be the jokester, the cool guy at parties. But as the years went by, his laughs got weird, and family gatherings turned into awkward, tense situations.

It's like this drink took control, turning him into a stumbling, tipsy robot. And it wasn't just his body—it messed with his brain too. Decisions that used to make sense became all random and messed up. There were these invisible regrets hanging around, making everything heavy and tense.

I know I mentioned this in the previous chapter. It's a flashback. One night, things got way out of hand. The relative, totally drunk, did something I can't unsee—he drank his own pee. Yeah, you heard it right. It was like he lost all control, this was a seriously messed-up moment that stuck with me.

But it's not just about that one weird incident; it's about how alcohol can flip a switch and turn people into someone else. Like, it's this secret side that comes out, and suddenly, everything's out of control. Let's talk about what this liquid rollercoaster can trigger.

1. Uninhibited Arguments: You've seen it, right? A little too much to drink, and suddenly, people are arguing about stuff that doesn't even matter. Friendships crumble, relationships break apart—all because of some unnecessary argument that got fueled by alcohol. Perhaps those who are heavy drinkers might consider not just a designated driver, but a designated communicator; someone to carry out a sober conversation on their behalf. That's just a thought, I wish I had earlier.

2. Loss of Friendships and Relationships:
It's not just arguments; it's about losing people. You say things you don't mean, do things you regret, and bam, friendships and relationships go down the drain. All because of a drink.

3. Career Woes: Imagine waking up with a killer hangover and realizing you messed up at work the night before. Maybe you said something to your boss or a colleague that you shouldn't have. Alcohol can mess with your career, and the consequences can be huge.

4. Mental Health Hits the Rocks: This one's serious. Too much drinking messes with your head. Anxiety, depression, it's like a storm in your mind. And it's not just mental health; physical health takes a hit too.

I'm not trying to judge your adult decisions regarding drinking as I am certain you will be guided by your own conscience. But seriously, let's think about this stuff. It's not just a drink; it's like a rollercoaster, and once you get on, you might not know where it's gonna take you. I can remember getting on a ride at an amusement park. The ride was called "Free Fall." Once a person is strapped in, there's no turning back, changing your mind. So, when the ride ended, never was I so happy to see the ground. I made up my mind that this would be my last ride at an amusement park, fair or any such place. I am fine enjoying the food and refreshments, for real.

I am keenly aware that more than a few people are using more than alcohol to change their mood, "mellow out," soothe the effects of bad news, or to overlook catastrophic crises that are too difficult to face. Judge yourself as to what you go to for relief. Perhaps marijuana, prescription meds, painkillers which can be highly addictive, or other illicit behaviors can take precedence over one's thought process and decision making. What began as a good idea can have devastating consequences. I am only saying this so that we are considering who besides ourselves is being affected by our choices. As this journey of being triggered unfolds, I will give potential strategies to deal responsibly with triggers.

Chapter 12: Responding to our Triggers

As I reflect on the intricate voyage through the complex landscape of triggers, I am reminded of the profound impact they have had on my life and the lives of those around me. I have learned that, some personality traits increase the individuals' vulnerability to symptoms of social anxiety, while others protect them (Macovei CM et al.2023). Triggers, those subtle yet powerful catalysts that awaken dormant emotions and memories, have been my chaperons through a major part of the intricate network of self-discovery. In this concluding chapter, I aim to encapsulate the essence of triggers or being triggered, reaffirm their significance, and explore a proactive approach to dealing with them. Through the lens of ICE—Identify, Communicate, and Edify—I seek to unravel the mysteries of triggers and pave the way for a more conscious and compassionate existence.

I. Identifying the Trigger:

Understanding triggers begins with self-awareness. It requires a courageous journey into the depths of our psyche, where buried emotions and memories lie dormant, awaiting resurrection. Identifying triggers is akin to holding a mirror to our inner selves, acknowledging the scars and wounds that have shaped us. The first step in the ICE approach is to Identify the trigger.

Triggers manifest in various forms—words, actions, smells, loss, victories, or even environments. Recognizing these triggers empowers us to confront our emotional baggage head-on. It requires introspection, an unwavering commitment to self-discovery, and a willingness to embrace vulnerability. Identifying triggers is not an act of weakness; rather, it is an act of strength and resilience, laying the foundation for personal growth and healing.

II. Communicating About It:

Once a trigger is identified, the next crucial step is communication. Silence, though tempting, perpetuates the cycle of emotional turbulence triggered by unaddressed wounds. First communicate with God in prayer being authentic. We can pray with confidence as we ask God according to His will to help us with whatever is causing us to be triggered. Please understand that effective communication is the bridge that connects the internal world of emotions with the external world of relationships. In the ICE framework, the 'C' represents Communicate about it.

Expressing our triggers to ourselves, to our God as people of faith, and to others is a transformative process. It fosters understanding, empathy, and connection. Communicating about triggers is not an admission of defeat but a declaration of our commitment to growth. By sharing our triggers, we dismantle the walls that isolate us from those around us, creating an environment conducive to healing. Discussing one's triggers is crucial to the success or demise of many human relationships. I have

made it a critical necessity to share with my

wife what triggers I have that she needs to be

aware of. While I have not served in military,

just growing up in Brooklyn has exposed me

to a different life from a cultural standpoint

than she had in the South. Not that one

environment is better, but certainly different,

and this difference being acknowledged and

validated mutually contributes to our happy

harmonious union. * A note for married or

engaged to be married couples; Please find a

means to communicate with each other about

what happened to you during and throughout

your childhood into adulthood. For example, if

you have been abandoned, abused,

assaulted, bullied, broken, or otherwise, you

definitely have some large opportunities to be

triggered by words, phrases, songs, aromas, pictures, movies, gestures, and environments. How you deal with these known triggers can minimize anxiety and quick-tempered actions.

III. Edify

The final stage of the ICE approach is to seek to *edify* (build up) every life we touch, especially those affected by our triggers. Edification involves not only personal growth but also a commitment to uplifting others. Triggers, when left unattended, can inadvertently harm those in our orbit. Seeking to edify is a conscious effort to minimize the collateral damage caused when we are triggered.

Edification extends beyond ourselves—it is a

ripple effect that touches the lives of those around us. By recognizing and addressing our triggers, we pave the way for healthier relationships, fostering an atmosphere of understanding, support, and compassion. In seeking to *edify*, we contribute to the collective well-being of our communities and create a positive impact that transcends individual experiences. You cannot build and break at the same time. Through the sharing of some of my personal experiences and through self-awareness, it is my prayer and hope that the information shared in these pages has in some way served to enhance the life of every reader.

Conclusion:

In concluding this exploration of triggers, I am

reminded that life is a continuous journey of self-discovery and growth. Triggers, rather than obstacles, are steppingstones toward a more authentic and fulfilled existence. The ICE approach—Identify, Communicate, and Edify—is a roadmap for navigating the complex web of triggers with grace and resilience.

As we traverse the intricate pathways of life, let us carry the lessons of triggers with us. Let us be vigilant in identifying the triggers that shape our emotional landscapes, courageous in communicating about them, and compassionate in seeking to *edify* every life we touch. In doing so, we not only enhance our own well-being but contribute to the collective fabric of human experience, weaving a narrative of understanding, empathy, and growth. While this publication in no way attempts to exhaust the magnitude of triggers, their causes, and effects, which some are indeed rooted in abuse, neglect, poverty and more, my prayer for the readers is: May your journey through triggers be not just a passage but a transformative odyssey toward a more enlightened and harmonious existence. If you are in need of counsel please do not hesitate to consult a professional counselor or therapist. The Lord bless and keep you, the Lord lift up His countenance upon you and be gracious unto you. May He give you peace in your heart, at home, in your life, at work, school or wherever your travels may find you, may you have the peace of God in Jesus name is my prayer.

Amen.

References:

dlo316. (2008, April 2). *The Pursuit of Happyness: Basketball scene* [Video]. YouTube. https://www.youtube.com/watch?v=ajjGtsjl7CM

James 3:5 (NIV). (n.d.). Bible Gateway. https://www.biblegateway.com/passage/NIV

Liu, G. S., Nguyen, B. L., Lyons, B. H., Sheats, K. J., Wilson, R. F., Betz, C. J., & Fowler, K. A. (2023). Surveillance for Violent Deaths — National Violent Death Reporting System, 48 states, the District of Columbia, and Puerto Rico, 2020. *Morbidity and Mortality Weekly Report, 72*(5), 1–38. https://doi.org/10.15585/mmwr.ss7205a1

Macovei CM, Bumbuc Ş, Martinescu-Bădălan F. *The role of personality traits in mediating the relation between fear of negative evaluation and social interaction anxiety.* Front Psychol. 2023 Oct 19;14:1268052. doi: 10.3389/fpsyg.2023.1268052. PMID: 37928579; PMCID: PMC10621049.

Pedersen, T. (2022, April 28). *What are triggers, and how do they form?* Psych Central. https://psychcentral.com/lib/what-is-a-trigger

Unless otherwise noted, all scriptures are taken from the King James Version of the Holy Bible.

www.ingramcontent.com/pod-product-compliance
Lightning Source LLC
Chambersburg PA
CBHW071030280326
41935CB00011B/1523